Patricia,
You will always be an honorary Trixie, so
never forget us!
Love, Debbie

Texas

WILD AND BEAUTIFUL

photography by WILLARD CLAY

FARCOUNTRY
PRESS

RIGHT: Agave at sunset, with a back-
drop of the Chisos Mountains.

FRONT COVER: Big Bend bluebonnets
below the Chisos Mountains.

BACK COVER: In Bastrop County.

TITLE PAGE: Fantastic eroded clay formations in Big Bend National Park.

ISBN 1-56037-217-6
Photographs © Willard Clay
© 2002 Farcountry Press

For more information on our books
write: Farcountry Press, P.O. Box 5630,
Helena, MT 59604 or call: (800) 654-1105
or visit montanamagazine.com

Created, produced, and designed in the
United States.
Printed in China

FOREWORD

1 was talking to a Texan visiting one of the state's many state parks and I asked him where he was from. His answer was, "I live about two hundred miles down the road." Two hundred miles down the road? I am currently living in northern Illinois and two hundred miles down the road to the west would put me in Des Moines, Iowa; two hundred miles to the north would be in Green Bay, Wisconsin; and two hundred miles to the east would be in Indianapolis, Indiana! The area of Texas exceeds one quarter of a million square miles. A land mass that size would hold 250 Rhode Islands!

When travelers enter the state at El Paso on Interstate 10, and they leave Interstate 10 at Louisiana, the highway markers exceed 900. Nine hundred miles to the south of where I live in Illinois is not far from New Orleans!

Because of the vastness of the state, another feature one notices is its diversity. The topographical changes are striking. There is the desert environment of west Texas near El Paso featuring the ubiquitous creosote bushes. East Texas has swamps with cypress trees, Big Bend National Park in south Texas features the towering Chisos Mountains and the Rio Grande River, the "Hill Country" of central Texas has some of the most beautiful shows of wild flowers when spring rain is abundant, and the panhandle has some of the most desolate grasslands in the country. And of course, Texas has an "ocean coastline" on the Gulf of Mexico. One of the most amazing sites is the miles and miles of uninhabited beach along the Padre Island Coast.

ABOVE: A Presidio County mission.
FACING PAGE: Mule Ears Peaks, Big Bend National Park.

Characteristics that appear to be truly "Texan" are the large cattle ranches, the number of oil wells scattered throughout the landscape, and the rolling hills of Texas bluebonnets, vast numbers of inland lakes and reservoirs, and countless miles of barbed wire fences. The state's history has produced features that are an integral part of Texas such as missions, especially those in San Antonio, county courthouse buildings located in most counties, Tex-Mex food, and Texas barbecue.

Another "Texas trait" that should be mentioned, especially in the ranch country of west Texas, is the courtesy Texas motorists display by waving as they meet each other on the roadways. One Texan said to me, "If I wave to you on the road and you don't wave back, that will make me angry."

Trying to capture all this flavor of Texas photographically in a reasonable amount of time is a Texas-size order; however, it is worth the effort. The state's diversity makes the project interesting and for traveling photographers needing a place to stop for the night, Texas has many well-equipped state parks. And finally, the hospitality of the state cannot be overlooked. As one Texan told me, "If you ask me for a dollar, I will give you two!"

WILLARD CLAY

ABOVE: Tupelo gum trees in Martin Dies, Jr., State Park, Jasper County.

FACING PAGE: El Capitan in Guadalupe Mountains National Park.

ABOVE: Door detail inside the Presidio, Fort Leaton State Historic Park.

FACING PAGE: Volcanic rocks scattered around a hedgehog cactus near Tuff Canyon, Big Bend National Park.

LEFT: Spicewood Spring feeds this stream that flows to the Colorado River in Colorado Bend State Park.

BELOW: Warnock's rock nettle abloom.

ABOVE: A new day begins on the Pease River of Hardeman and Foard counties.

FACING PAGE: Enchanted Rock State Park, Gillespie County, protects sandstone formations like these.

ABOVE: A storm moves in over Rita Blanca National Grassland, Dallam County.

LEFT: This boulder field lies below El Capitan in Culberson County.

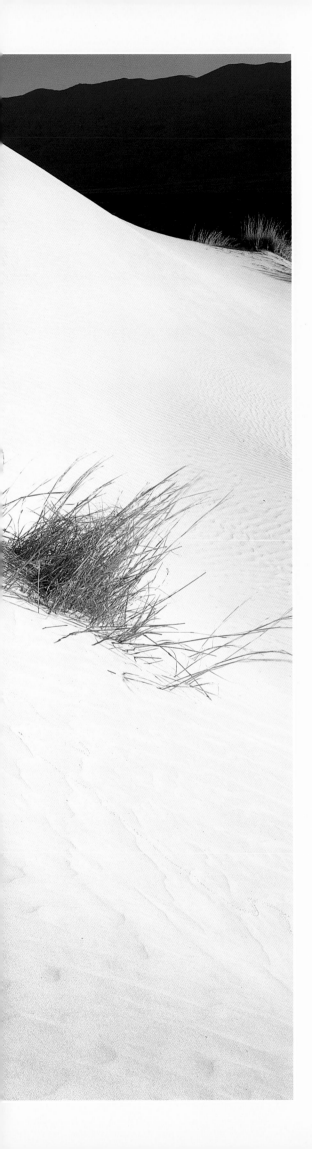

ABOVE: Saint Steven's Episcopal Church in Fort Stockton dates from 1896.

LEFT: Gypsum dunes below the Guadalupe Mountains.

ABOVE: Sunset colors storm clouds that boil over the Gypsum Dunes.

FACING PAGE: Falls and water pockets in Pedernales Falls State Park.

RIGHT: Heliotrope adorns Monahans Sandhills State Park, Ward County.

BELOW: Sunset at El Capitan.

FACING PAGE: Where the Pecos and Rio Grande rivers meet, in Amistad National Recreation Area.

RIGHT: Night falls near Belmont.

BELOW: In Brisco County, Caprock Canyons State Park is filled with wonders.

ABOVE: Shades of autumn brighten McKittrick Canyon, part of the Chihuahuan Desert ecosystem in Culberson County.

LEFT: Remains of the Johnson Ranch on River Road in Big Bend National Park.

Safely in harbor at Corpus Christie.
RICHARD REYNOLDS

FACING PAGE: The hardy prickly pear cactus grows out of lichen-covered sandstone on Enchanted Rock in its namesake state park.

BELOW: Luckenbach's post office.

ABOVE: Grasslands near Silverton.

RIGHT: This stone wall near Comfort in the Hill Country was a long time abuilding.

Lucheguilla, a succulent, flourishes amid volcanic rock near Tuff Canyon.

LEFT: Pink ladies cover a field in Wilson County.

BELOW: Sunrise on the vacation haven of Padre Island National Seashore in the Gulf of Mexico.

FACING PAGE: Sotol, prickly pear, and lechuguilla.

BELOW: In Palmetto State Park, Gonzales County, visitors admire these dwarf palmetto palms.

FACING PAGE: One perfect yucca blossom below Goat Mountain.

ABOVE: Prickly pear cactus blossoms are some compensation for the plant's needle-like spines.

LEFT: Shrimp boats rest up from their labors in Aransas County's Conn Brown Harbor.

ABOVE: The officers quarters is one of twenty original building remaining at Fort Concho National Historic Landmark, San Angelo, dating from 1867 when it was manned to protect West Texas settlers. RICHARD REYNOLDS

FACING PAGE: A freezing touch to the South Prong of the Little Red River.

Swampland in Caddo Lake State Park.

FACING PAGE: Bluebonnets, the Texas state flower, dominate a field near near Gillett.

BELOW: Sundown over the Gulf of Mexico, viewed from the Kleberg County shore.

ABOVE: Bald cypress tree trunk sculpture beside the Guadalupe River.

FACING PAGE: Mud plates bordering the Rio Grande.

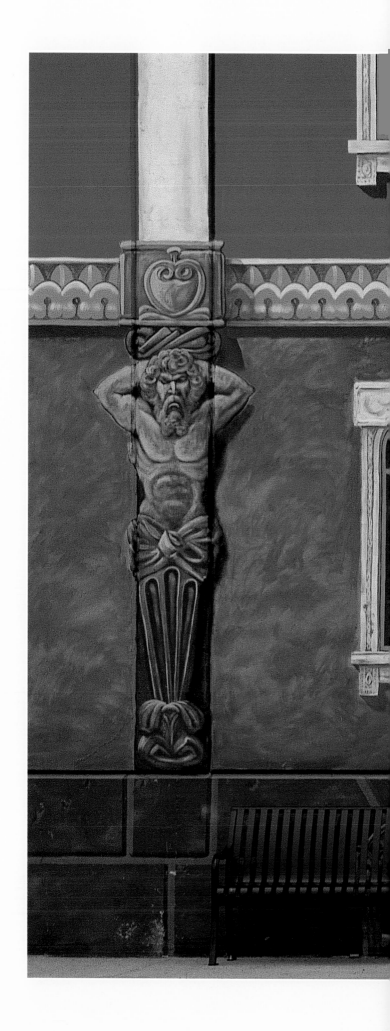

ABOVE: Drummond's phlox color the land near Gonzales.

RIGHT: Trompe l'oeil architectural detail enlivens Lubbock's historic depot district. JOHN REDDY

FACING PAGE: Prairie Dog Town Fork of the Red River in Palo Duro Canyon State Park.

BELOW: The Texas longhorn, one of the world's most famous cattle breeds. RICHARD REYNOLDS

ABOVE: Ice and fog mute the Chisos Mountains landscape.

LEFT: Santa Elena Canyon on the Rio Grande.

ABOVE: Mission San Juan Capistrano in San Antonio.

RIGHT: The shrimping industry is Texas' largest commercial fishing business, and the state has ranked in the top three nationally for five decades of shrimp harvesting.

ABOVE: Visitors view area frontier artifacts inside the 1870s house of Frijole Ranch Historic Site in Guadalupe Mountains National Park.

RIGHT: Sunset's afterglow illuminates Sabine County's Toledo Bend Reservoir at Indian Mounds.

Oxbow Lake is a feature of Bentsen–Rio Grande State Park.

FACING PAGE: Peaceful reflections along Oak Creek, Big Bend National Park.

BELOW: Lesser sandhill cranes at Lower Pauls Lake in the Muleshoe National Wildlife Refuge.

LEFT: Dogwood blossoms signal springtime in Cassells/Boykin State Park.

BELOW: Gorman Falls in Colorado Bend State Park.

RIGHT: Llano County barn and sky.

BELOW: The romantically-named claret cup cactus.

A sign of settlement
beyond High Plains
buttes near Crosbyton.

ABOVE: After the storm at Umbarger..

RIGHT: The Alamo in San Antonio, revered symbol of Texas independence.

ABOVE: Fort Leaton, today a historic park, began life as an adobe trading post serving the Apache and Comanche in 1848.

FACING PAGE: Oil wells in Lake Arrowhead.

RIGHT: Storm clouds over the Rio Grande near Redford.

BELOW: These huecos (waterholes) in Hueco Tanks State Park, El Paso Country, have been filled by a summer rain.

LEFT: Wild horse roundup in Guadalupe Mountains National Park.
RICHARD REYNOLDS

BELOW: Fort Stockton's historic Riggs Hotel was built in 1904 to serve stagecoach passengers, and now is a museum holding original furnishings and gear.

ABOVE: Windmill at work in Rita Blanca National Grasslands, Dallam County.

LEFT: Sunset above a High Plains horizon in Crosby County.

Loop Camp sunrise on the Rio Grande.

FACING PAGE: A dead juniper tree stands sentinel above eroded clay in Palo Duro Canyon State Park.

RIGHT: Sea shell still life, Padre Island.

BELOW: Javelina is the Spanish name for the peccary, also called wild boar. TOM BEAN

ABOVE: The yellow of butterweed and the brilliance of purple ground cherry.

FACING PAGE: Colorful craft for sailing the Gulf of Mexico. RICHARD REYNOLDS

ABOVE: Lake Daingerfield, Harrison County, covered with lily pads.

LEFT: The barn at future President Johnson's boyhood home, Lyndon Johnson National Historic Park.

FACING PAGE: Pillars of strength: an oak tree fronts the Greater First Baptist Church in Anderson.

BELOW: Caddo Lake reflects cypress trees.

FACING PAGE: Cypress trees in Big Thicket National Preserve, Hardin County.

BELOW: Lotuses adorn a Fannin County pond.

FACING PAGE: Waiting for a cowboy in Denton County.

BELOW: Prickly pear cactus and loblolly pine cones in Bastrop State Park.

ABOVE: Justice and juice were served up by Judge Roy Bean in his Jersey Lilly Saloon, Langtry.

FACING PAGE: Sunset spotlights a sotol.

RIGHT: McKinney Falls, Onion Creek, in Travis County.

BELOW: A western diamondback rattlesnake in action.   RUTH HOYT

FACING PAGE: Twin delights at Gorman Falls.

BELOW: Red River Valley hay rolls near Omaha.

LEFT: Downtown Dallas as seen from the west. RICHARD REYNOLDS

BELOW: Rainbow cactus in flower.

99

LEFT: Historic wagon—with ornamentation—at Fort Leaton State Historical Park.

BELOW: Along their Camino Real ("royal highway") near today's city of El Paso, the Spanish founded Nuestra Señora de la Purísima Concepción del Socorro in the 1680s.

ABOVE: Texas' state bird, the mockingbird. RUTH HOYT

RIGHT: The Fulton Mansion State Historic Structure at Rockport dates from 1877 and was built to withstand hurricanes.

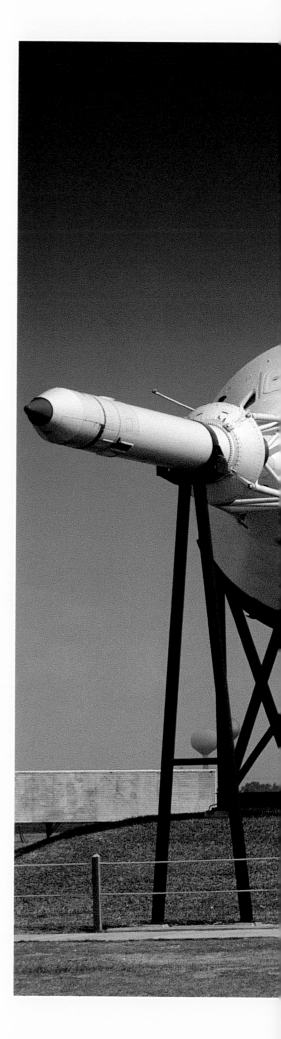

ABOVE: Galveston's beach front. RICHARD REYNOLDS

RIGHT: Outdoor exhibits are only part of what visitors see at Houston's
Lyndon B. Johnson Space Center, a NASA installation. RICHARD REYNOLDS

The Rio Grande at Hot Springs.

FACING PAGE: Gentle evening sun highlights Rio Grande boulders in Presidio County.

BELOW: Directly translated from Spanish, "armadillo" means little armed one, for this nocturnal animal's bony surface plates. TOM BEAN

FACING PAGE: The Davis Mountains in Jeff Davis County.

BELOW: Cleburn State Park.

ABOVE: The second-largest state's shape, at Burkburnett.

LEFT: Cypress trees and knees.

FACING PAGE: Mormon tea, lechuguilla, and prickly pears.

BELOW: A Texas horned lizard. RUTH HOYT

ABOVE: Cypress trees in their fall colors.

LEFT: At Henderson, a persimmon tree nears harvest in the autumn.

FACING PAGE: Fresh paint for a Jeff Davis County ranch.

RIGHT: Autumn-tinted sumac in Nacogdoches County.

BELOW: The restored Fort Worth Stock Exchange in the Stockyard Historic District now houses shops and restaurants. JOHN REDDY

The rocking source of so much Texas wealth; this one near Denver City.